THE *Skinny*
NUTRiBULLET
MEALS IN MINUTES
RECIPE BOOK

 CookNation

THE SKINNY NUTRIBULLET MEALS IN MINUTES RECIPE BOOK

QUICK & EASY, SINGLE SERVING SUPPERS, SNACKS, SAUCES, SALAD DRESSINGS & MORE USING YOUR NUTRIBULLET. ALL UNDER 300, 400 & 500 CALORIES

ISBN 978-1-909855-65-6

A CIP catalogue record of this book is available from the British Library

DISCLAIMER

This book is designed to provide information on meals, snacks, sauces and salad dressings that can be made in the NUTRiBULLET appliance only, results may differ if alternative devices are used. The NutriBullet™ is a registered trademark of Homeland Housewares, LLC. Bell & Mackenzie Publishing is not affiliated with the owner of the trademark and is not an authorized distributor of the trademark owner's products or services.

This publication has not been prepared, approved, or licensed by NutriBullet ™ or Homeland Housewares, LLC.

Some recipes may contain nuts or traces of nuts. Those suffering from any allergies associated with nuts should avoid any recipes containing nuts or nut based oils.

This information is provided and sold with the knowledge that the publisher and author do not offer any legal or other professional advice.

In the case of a need for any such expertise consult with the appropriate professional.

This book does not contain all information available on the subject, and other sources of recipes are available.

This book has not been created to be specific to any individual's or NUTRiBULLET's requirements.

Every effort has been made to make this book as accurate as possible. However, there may be typographical and or content errors. Therefore, this book should serve only as a general guide and not as the ultimate source of subject information.

This book contains information that might be dated and is intended only to educate and entertain.

The author and publisher shall have no liability or responsibility to any person or entity regarding any loss or damage incurred, or alleged to have incurred, directly or indirectly, by the information contained in this book.

CONTENTS

You may also enjoy.....

80+ DELICIOUS & NUTRITIOUS HEALTHY SMOOTHIE RECIPES. BURN FAT, LOSE WEIGHT AND FEEL GREAT!

ISBN 978-1-909855-57-1

DELICIOUS, QUICK & EASY, SINGLE SERVING SOUPS & PASTA SAUCES FOR YOUR NUTRIBULLET. ALL UNDER 100, 200, 300 & 400 CALORIES

ISBN 978-1-909855-59-5

INTRODUCTION

Push the boundaries of your NUTRiBULLET and use it to create delicious, nutritious, low calorie meals in minutes!

If you love your NUTRiBULLET, not only can you make great-tasting smoothies and delicious soups but now you can create super-fast, simple, single serving meals, snacks, sauces, salad dressings and more. With our recipes and your NUTRiBULLET, mealtime prep is fast and fun with much less washing up. If time is your enemy or you are managing your weight as part of a calorie controlled diet our recipes are your perfect companion. Each of the skinny dishes are calorie counted below either 300, 400 or 500 calories, most can be prepared and cooked in around 15 minutes or less and all make use of your NUTRiBULLET.

The NUTRiBULLET can do so much more than just make smoothies. There's no need to spend hours in the kitchen or complicated culinary techniques, speedy suppers can be just minutes away.

Our skinny recipes are tasty and healthy using fresh and seasonal ingredients where possible and all use the power of the NUTRiBULLET to extract the goodness from each ingredient, unlocking the powerful nutrients for our bodies to absorb and use without compromising on flavour.

The recipes in this book are all written for use with the NUTRiBULLET but can also be used with other blenders.

You may also enjoy:

The Skinny NUTRiBULLET Soup Recipe Book
Delicious, Quick & Easy, Single Serving Soups & Pasta Sauces For Your Nutribullet. All Under 100, 200, 300 & 400 Calories. Click here.

The Skinny NUTRiBULLET Recipe Book
80+ Delicious & Nutritious Healthy Smoothie Recipes. Burn Fat, Lose Weight and Feel Great! Click here.

SKINNY RECIPES

The recipes in this book are all low calorie dishes for one, which will make it easier for you to monitor your overall daily calorie intake as well as those you are cooking for. The recommended daily calories are approximately 2000 for women and 2500 for men.

Broadly speaking, by consuming the recommended levels of calories each day you should maintain your current weight. Reducing the number of calories (a calorie deficit) will result in losing weight. This happens because the body begins to use fat stores for energy to make up the reduction in calories, which in turn results in weight loss. We have already counted the calories for each dish making it easy for you to fit this into your daily eating plan whether you want to lose weight, maintain your current figure or are just looking for some great-tasting, comforting, winter warming recipes.

All the recipes in this book are a guide only. You may need to alter quantities and cooking times to suit your own appliances.

I'M ALREADY ON A DIET. CAN I USE THESE RECIPES?

Yes of course. All the recipes can be great accompaniments to many of the popular calorie-counting diets. We all know that sometimes dieting can result in hunger pangs, cravings and boredom from eating the same old foods day in and day out. Skinny NUTRiBULLET Meals In Minutes provide filling recipes that should satisfy you for hours afterwards.

NUTRITION

All of the recipes in this collection are balanced low calorie meals that should keep you feeling full. It is important to balance your food between proteins, good carbs, dairy, fruit and vegetables.

• **Protein.** Keeps you feeling full and is also essential for building body tissue. Good protein sources come from meat, fish and eggs.

• **Carbohydrates.** Not all carbs are good and generally they are high in calories, which makes them difficult to include in a calorie limiting diet. However carbs are a good source of energy for your body as they are converted more easily into glucose (sugar) providing energy. Try to eat 'good carbs' which are high in fibre and nutrients e.g. whole fruits and veg, nuts, seeds, whole grain cereals, beans and legumes.

• **Dairy.** Dairy products provide you with vitamins and minerals. Cheeses can be very high in calories but other products such as low fat Greek yoghurt, crème fraiche and skimmed milk are all good.

• **Fruit & Vegetables.** Eat your five a day. There is never a better time to fill your 5 a day quota. Not only are fruit and veg very healthy, they also fill up your plate and are ideal snacks when you are feeling hungry.

SKINNY TIPS

If you are following a diet or generally keeping an eye on your calorie intake, here are some tips that will help you manage the way you eat.

In today's fast moving society many of use have adopted an unhealthy habit of eating. We eat as quickly as possibly without properly giving our bodies the chance to digest and feel full. Not only is this bad for your digestive system, but our bodies begin to relate food to just fuel instead of actually enjoying what we are eating.

Some simple tips for eating which may help you on your fasting days:

- Eat. Take it slow. There is no rush.
- Chew. It sounds obvious but you should properly chew your food and swallow only when it's broken down and you have enjoyed what you have tasted.
- Wait. Before reaching for second helpings wait 5-10 minutes and let your body tell you whether you are still hungry. More often than not, the answer will be no and you will be satisfied with the meal you have had. A glass of water before each meal will help you with any cravings for more.
- Avoid alcohol when you can. Alcohol is packed with calories and will counter affect any calorific reduction you are practising with your daily meals.
- Drink plenty of water throughout the day. It's good for you, has zero calories, and will fill you up and help stop you feeling hungry.
- Drink a glass of water before and also with your meal. Again this will help you feel fuller.
- When you are eating each meal, put your fork down between bites – it will make you eat more slowly and you'll feel fuller on less food.
- Brush your teeth immediately after your meal to discourage yourself from eating more.
- If unwanted food cravings do strike, acknowledge them, then distract yourself. Go out for a walk, phone a friend, play with the kids, or paint your nails.
- Whenever hunger hits, try waiting 15 minutes and ride out the cravings. You'll find they pass and you can move on with your day
- Remember - feeling a bit hungry is not a bad thing. We are all so used to acting on the smallest hunger pangs that we forget what it's like to feel genuinely hungry. Learn to 'own' your hunger and take control of how you deal with it.
- Get moving. Increased activity will complement your weight loss efforts. Think about what you are doing each day: choose the stairs instead of the lift, walk to the shops instead of driving. Making small changes will not only help you burn calories but will make you feel healthier and more in control of your weight loss.

CLEANING YOUR NUTRIBULLET

Cleaning the NUTRiBULLET is thankfully very easy. The manufacturer gives clear guidelines on how best to do this but here's a recap:

- Make sure the NUTRiBULLET is unplugged before disassembling or cleaning.
- Set aside the power base and blade holders as these should not be used in a dishwasher.
- Use hot soapy water to clean the blades but do not immerse in boiling water as this can warp the plastic.
- Use a damp cloth to clean the power base.
- All cups and lids can be placed in a dishwasher.
- For stubborn marks inside the cup, fill the cup 2/3 full of warm soapy water and screw on the milling blade. Attached to the power base and run for 20-30 seconds.
- Warning:
- Do not put your hands or any utensils near the moving blade. Always ensure the NUTRiBULLET is unplugged when assembling/disassembling or cleaning.

ABOUT COOKNATION

CookNation is the leading publisher of innovative and practical recipe books for the modern, health-conscious cook.

CookNation titles bring together delicious, easy and practical recipes with their unique approach, making cooking for diets and healthy eating fast, simple and fun.

With a range of #1 best-selling titles - from the innovative 'Skinny' calorie-counted series, to the 5:2 Diet Recipes Collection - CookNation recipe books prove that 'Diet' can still mean 'Delicious'!

Turn to the end of this book to browse all CookNation's recipe books.

 **CookNation**

Skinny
PASTA
MEALS IN MINUTES

Feel free to double the quantities to cook for more people. All of these recipes include a 75g/3oz serving of dry pasta (270 calories). Spaghetti, Linguine, Penne or any dried, ideally wholewheat, pasta work for any recipe.

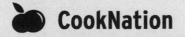

CHERRY TOMATO & OLIVE PASTA SAUCE

380 calories per serving

Ingredients

- 150g/5oz cherry tomatoes
- 25g/1oz pitted black olives
- 1 tsp anchovy paste or 1 anchovy fillet
- 1 tsp olive oil

- Small handful of basil leaves
- ½ garlic clove, peeled
- 75g/3oz dried pasta
- Salt & pepper to taste

Method

1 Add the pasta to a pan of salted boiling water and cook until tender.

2 Add the rest of the ingredients to the NUTRiBULLET tall cup. Be careful the ingredients don't go past the MAX line on your machine.

3 Twist on the NUTRiBULLET blade, turn the cup over and give it a tap down to make sure all the ingredients fall onto the blade. Attach to the NUTRiBULLET power base and pulse for one second at a time to give you a textured sauce. Don't blend for too long, as you don't want to end up with a pureed sauce.

4 Scoop out the sauce and toss with the hot drained pasta. Season and serve.

CHEFS NOTE
Linguine is a good pasta choice for this simple sauce.

FRESH SPINACH & PARMESAN PASTA SAUCE

480 calories per serving

Ingredients

- 75g/3oz spinach
- 25g/1oz pine nuts
- 1 tbsp olive oil
- 2 tbsp water (use a little more if needed)

- 1 tbsp grated Parmesan cheese
- 75g/3oz dried pasta
- Salt & pepper to taste

Method

1 Add the pasta to a pan of salted boiling water and cook until tender.

2 Add the rest of the ingredients to the NUTRiBULLET tall cup. Be careful the ingredients don't go past the MAX line on your machine.

3 Twist on the NUTRiBULLET blade, turn the cup over and give it a tap down to make sure all the ingredients fall onto the blade. Attach to the NUTRiBULLET power base and pulse for one second at a time to make a paste. Don't blend for too long, as you don't want to end up with a very smooth pureed sauce.

4 Scoop out the sauce and toss with the hot drained pasta. Season and serve.

CHEFS NOTE

Add a little fresh basil if you have it and try serving with a splash of balsamic vinegar.

13

GREEN PESTO PASTA SAUCE

460 calories per serving

Ingredients

- 50g/2oz fresh basil
- 1 garlic clove, peeled
- 25g/1oz pine nuts
- 1 tbsp olive oil
- 2 tbsp water (use a little more if needed)
- 1 tbsp grated Parmesan cheese
- 75g/3oz dried pasta
- Salt & pepper to taste

Method

1 Add the pasta to a pan of salted boiling water and cook until tender.

2 Add the rest of the ingredients to the NUTRiBULLET tall cup. Be careful the ingredients don't go past the MAX line on your machine.

3 Twist on the NUTRiBULLET blade, turn the cup over and give it a tap down to make sure all the ingredients fall onto the blade. Attach to the NUTRiBULLET power base and pulse for one second at a time to make a paste. Don't blend for too long, as you don't want to end up with a very smooth pureed sauce.

4 Scoop out the sauce and toss with the hot drained pasta. Season and serve.

CHEFS NOTE

If you have time - toast the pine nuts by warming them in a dry frying pan until they begin to gently brown.

PARSLEY & FETA CHEESE PASTA SAUCE

470 calories per serving

Ingredients

- 50g/2oz low fat feta cheese
- 50g/2oz fresh flat leaf parsley
- 1 garlic clove, peeled
- 1 tbsp pine nuts
- 1 tsp olive oil
- 2 tbsp water (use a little more if needed)
- 75g/3oz dried pasta
- Salt & pepper to taste

Method

1 Add the pasta to a pan of salted boiling water and cook until tender.

2 Add the rest of the ingredients to the NUTRiBULLET tall cup. Be careful the ingredients don't go past the MAX line on your machine.

3 Twist on the NUTRiBULLET blade, turn the cup over and give it a tap down to make sure all the ingredients fall onto the blade. Attach to the NUTRiBULLET power base and pulse for one second at a time to make a paste. Don't blend for too long, as you don't want to end up with a very smooth pureed sauce.

4 Scoop out the sauce and toss with the hot drained pasta. Season and serve.

CHEFS NOTE
You could try mint rather than parsley, or a mixture of both.

SUNDRIED TOMATO PASTA SAUCE

420 calories per serving

Ingredients

- 75g/3oz sundried tomatoes, drained
- 1 garlic clove, peeled
- 1 handful of fresh basil
- 1 tbsp grated Parmesan cheese
- 75g/3oz dried pasta
- Salt & pepper to taste

TRY SUNDRIED PASTE

Method

1 Add the pasta to a pan of salted boiling water and cook until tender.

2 Add the rest of the ingredients to the NUTRiBULLET tall cup. Be careful the ingredients don't go past the MAX line on your machine.

3 Twist on the NUTRiBULLET blade, turn the cup over and give it a tap down to make sure all the ingredients fall onto the blade. Attach to the NUTRiBULLET power base and pulse for one second at a time to make a paste. (Use a little water if you need to loosen the sauce up during blending). Don't blend for too long, as you don't want to end up with a very smooth pureed sauce.

4 Scoop out the sauce and toss with the hot drained pasta. Season and serve.

CHEFS NOTE
Jars of sundried tomatoes are available everywhere, drain the oil off and add a little water if the sauce needs loosening up.

ALMOND & SULTANA PASTA SAUCE

449 calories per serving

Ingredients

- 3 vine-ripened plum tomatoes, halved
- 1 tbsp sultanas
- 1 tbsp blanched almonds
- ½ garlic clove, peeled
- 1 tbsp fresh basil

- 1 tsp olive oil
- 1 tsp anchovy paste or 1 anchovy fillet
- 75g/3oz dried pasta
- Salt & pepper to taste

Method

1 Add the pasta to a pan of salted boiling water and cook until tender.

2 Add the rest of the ingredients to the NUTRiBULLET tall cup. Be careful the ingredients don't go past the MAX line on your machine.

3 Twist on the NUTRiBULLET blade, turn the cup over and give it a tap down to make sure all the ingredients fall onto the blade. Attach to the NUTRiBULLET power base and pulse for one second at a time to make a paste. Don't blend for too long, as you don't want to end up with a very smooth pureed sauce.

4 Scoop out the sauce and toss with the hot drained pasta. Season and serve.

CHEFS NOTE
Reserve a little of the drained pasta water to use for loosening up the sauce if needed.

SMOOTH VEGETABLE & TOMATO SAUCE

370 calories per serving

Ingredients

- 150g/5oz cherry tomatoes, halved
- 1 garlic clove, crushed
- 1 carrot, finely chopped
- 1 celery stalk, chopped
- ½ tsp each salt & brown sugar

- 75g/3oz dried pasta
- 1 tsp grated Parmesan cheese
- Low cal cooking oil spray
- Salt & pepper to taste

Method

1 In a frying pan gently sauté the cherry tomatoes, garlic, carrot, celery, salt & sugar in a little low cal spray for about 10-15 minutes or until everything is nicely softened and combined. Remove from the heat, and leave to cool for a little while.

2 Meanwhile place the pasta in a pan of salted boiling water and cook until tender.

3 Now add the contents of the frying pan to the NUTRiBULLET tall cup. Be careful the ingredients don't go past the MAX line on your machine.

4 Twist on the NUTRiBULLET blade, turn the cup over and give it a tap down to make sure all the ingredients fall onto the blade. Attach to the NUTRiBULLET power base and pulse until smooth.

5 Scoop out the sauce and toss with the hot drained pasta in a pan. Alter the consistency by adding a little water if needed. Reheat, check the seasoning, sprinkle with Parmesan and serve.

(Please note: Per our method, the manufacturers of the NUTRiBULLET recommend you allow ingredients to cool before adding to the tall cup to avoid any heat damage to parts. Some people choose not to follow this recommendation and add the hot ingredients to the NUTRiBULLET and blend immediately for a ready-to-eat pasta sauce).

CHILLI TENDERSTEM BROCCOLI

380 calories per serving

Ingredients

- ¼ onion, chopped
- 1 garlic clove, crushed
- 2 tsp anchovy paste or 2 anchovy fillets
- 150g/5oz tenderstem broccoli/broccolini, chopped
- ½ red chilli, deseeded & sliced
- 75g/3oz dried pasta
- 1 tsp grated Parmesan cheese
- Low cal cooking oil spray
- Salt & pepper to taste

Method

1 In a frying pan gently sauté the onion, garlic & anchovy paste in a little low cal spray for 5 minutes (add a little water to the pan if needed). Now add the broccoli and chilli and cook for a further 10 minutes or until everything is nicely softened and combined. Remove from the heat, and leave to cool for a little while.

2 Meanwhile place the pasta in a pan of salted boiling water and cook until tender.

3 Now add the contents of the frying pan to the NUTRiBULLET tall cup. Be careful the ingredients don't go past the MAX line on your machine.

4 Twist on the NUTRiBULLET blade, turn the cup over and give it a tap down to make sure all the ingredients fall onto the blade. Attach to the NUTRiBULLET power base and pulse for one second at a time to give you a textured sauce.

(Add a little water if you need to loosen the sauce up). Don't blend for too long, as you don't want to end up with a pureed sauce.

5 Scoop out the broccoli and toss with the hot drained pasta in a pan. Alter the consistency by adding more water if needed. Reheat, check the seasoning and serve sprinkled with Parmesan cheese.

(Please note: Per our method, the manufacturers of the NUTRiBULLET recommend you allow ingredients to cool before adding to the tall cup to avoid any heat damage to parts. Some people choose not to follow this recommendation and add the hot ingredients to the NUTRiBULLET and blend immediately for a ready-to-eat pasta sauce).

ARRABIATA

340 calories per serving

Ingredients

- 150g/5oz tinned chopped tomatoes
- 1 garlic clove, crushed
- 1 red chilli, deseeded & sliced
- ½ tsp each salt & brown sugar

- 75g/3oz dried pasta
- 1 tsp grated Parmesan cheese
- Low cal cooking oil spray
- Salt & pepper to taste

Method

1 In a frying pan gently sauté tomatoes, garlic, chilli, salt & sugar in a little low cal spray for about 8-10 minutes or until everything is nicely softened and combined. Remove from the heat, and leave to cool for a little while.

2 Meanwhile place the pasta in a pan of salted boiling water and cook until tender.

3 Now add the contents of the frying pan to the NUTRiBULLET tall cup. Be careful the ingredients don't go past the MAX line on your machine.

4 Twist on the NUTRiBULLET blade, turn the cup over and give it a tap down to make sure all the ingredients fall onto the blade. Attach to the NUTRiBULLET power base and pulse until smooth.

5 Scoop out the sauce and toss with the hot drained pasta in a pan. Alter the consistency by adding a little water if needed. Reheat, check the seasoning, sprinkle with Parmesan and serve.

CHEFS NOTE
Penne is the traditional pasta shape to serve with arrabiata.

(Please note: Per our method, the manufacturers of the NUTRiBULLET recommend you allow ingredients to cool before adding to the tall cup to avoid any heat damage to parts. Some people choose not to follow this recommendation and add the hot ingredients to the NUTRiBULLET and blend immediately for a ready-to-eat pasta sauce).

CREAMY COURGETTE SAUCE

340 calories per serving

Ingredients

- 1 large courgette/zucchini, sliced
- ½ onion, chopped
- 1 garlic clove, crushed
- 2 tbsp low fat cream
- 75g/3oz dried pasta
- 1 tsp grated Parmesan cheese
- Low cal cooking oil spray
- Salt & pepper to taste

Method

1 In a frying pan gently sauté the courgette, onion & garlic in a little low cal spray for about 10 minutes or until everything is nicely softened and combined (add a little water to the pan if needed). Remove from the heat, and leave to cool for a little while.

2 Meanwhile place the pasta in a pan of salted boiling water and cook until tender.

3 Now add the contents of the frying pan to the NUTRiBULLET tall cup along with the cream. Be careful the ingredients don't go past the MAX line on your machine.

4 Twist on the NUTRiBULLET blade, turn the cup over and give it a tap down to make sure all the ingredients fall onto the blade. Attach to the NUTRiBULLET power base and pulse until smooth.

5 Scoop out the sauce and toss with the hot drained pasta in a pan. Alter the consistency by adding a little water if needed. Reheat, check the seasoning, sprinkle with Parmesan and serve.

CHEFS NOTE
Serve with lots of freshly ground black pepper.

(Please note: Per our method, the manufacturers of the NUTRiBULLET recommend you allow ingredients to cool before adding to the tall cup to avoid any heat damage to parts. Some people choose not to follow this recommendation and add the hot ingredients to the NUTRiBULLET and blend immediately for a ready-to-eat pasta sauce).

SMOOTH BUTTERNUT SQUASH SAUCE

407 calories per serving

Ingredients

- 125g/4oz butternut squash, peeled, de-seeded & finely chopped
- ½ onion, chopped
- 1 garlic clove, crushed
- 60ml/¼ cup water
- 2 tbsp low fat cream
- 75g/3oz dried pasta
- 1 tsp grated Parmesan cheese
- Low cal cooking oil spray
- Salt & pepper to taste

Method

1 In a frying pan gently sauté the squash, onion & garlic in a little low cal spray for 3-4 minutes. Add the water, increase the heat and cook for a further 10 minutes or until everything is nicely softened and combined. Remove from the heat, and leave to cool for a little while.

2 Meanwhile place the pasta in a pan of salted boiling water and cook until tender.

3 Now add the contents of the frying pan to the NUTRiBULLET tall cup along with the cream. Be careful the ingredients don't go past the MAX line on your machine.

4 Twist on the NUTRiBULLET blade, turn the cup over and give it a tap down to make sure all the ingredients fall onto the blade. Attach to the NUTRiBULLET power base and pulse until smooth.

5 Scoop out the sauce and toss with the hot drained pasta in a pan. Alter the consistency by adding a little water if needed. Reheat, check the seasoning, sprinkle with Parmesan and serve.

CHEFS NOTE

Any squash or pumpkin variety will work just as well in this recipe.

(Please note: Per our method, the manufacturers of the NUTRiBULLET recommend you allow ingredients to cool before adding to the tall cup to avoid any heat damage to parts. Some people choose not to follow this recommendation and add the hot ingredients to the NUTRiBULLET and blend immediately for a ready-to-eat pasta sauce).

CHESTNUT MUSHROOM PASTA SAUCE

395 calories per serving

Ingredients

- 125g/4oz chestnut mushrooms, sliced
- ½ onion, chopped
- 1 garlic clove, crushed
- 2 tbsp chopped flat leaf parsley
- 3 tbsp low fat cream
- 75g/3oz dried pasta
- 1 tsp grated Parmesan cheese
- Low cal cooking oil spray
- Salt & pepper to taste

Method

1 In a frying pan gently sauté the mushrooms, onion, garlic & parsley in a little low cal spray for about 10 minutes or until everything is nicely softened and combined. Remove from the heat, and leave to cool for a little while.

2 Meanwhile place the pasta in a pan of salted boiling water and cook until tender.

3 Now add the contents of the frying pan to the NUTRiBULLET tall cup along with the cream. Be careful the ingredients don't go past the MAX line on your machine.

4 Twist on the NUTRiBULLET blade, turn the cup over and give it a tap down to make sure all the ingredients fall onto the blade. Attach to the NUTRiBULLET power base and pulse until smooth.

5 Scoop out the sauce and toss with the hot drained pasta in a hot pan. Alter the consistency by adding a little water if needed. Reheat, check the seasoning, sprinkle with Parmesan and serve.

CHEFS NOTE
Don't worry if you don't have fresh parsley. Just add some dried mixed herbs or thyme.

(Please note: Per our method, the manufacturers of the NUTRiBULLET recommend you allow ingredients to cool before adding to the tall cup to avoid any heat damage to parts. Some people choose not to follow this recommendation and add the hot ingredients to the NUTRiBULLET and blend immediately for a ready-to-eat pasta sauce).

23

CRAB SAUCE

485 calories per serving

Ingredients

- 125g/4oz tinned crabmeat, drained
- ½ onion, chopped
- 1 garlic clove, crushed
- ½ red chilli deseeded & chopped
- 3 tbsp white wine
- 2 tbsp low fat cream
- 2 tbsp chopped flat leaf parsley
- 75g/3oz dried pasta
- Low cal cooking oil spray
- Salt & pepper to taste

Method

1 In a frying pan gently sauté the crabmeat, onion, garlic, chilli & wine in a little low cal spray for about 8-10 minutes or until everything is nicely softened and combined. Remove from the heat, and leave to cool for a little while.

2 Meanwhile place the pasta in a pan of salted boiling water and cook until tender.

3 Now add the contents of the frying pan to the NUTRiBULLET tall cup along with the cream. Be careful the ingredients don't go past the MAX line on your machine.

4 Twist on the NUTRiBULLET blade, turn the cup over and give it a tap down to make sure all the ingredients fall onto the blade. Attach to the NUTRiBULLET power base and pulse until smooth.

5 Scoop out the sauce and toss with the hot drained pasta in a pan. Alter the consistency by adding a little water if needed. Reheat, check the seasoning, sprinkle with parsley and serve.

CHEFS NOTE

Try adding some extra crabmeat to the sauce and pasta after it's been tossed.

(Please note: Per our method, the manufacturers of the NUTRiBULLET recommend you allow ingredients to cool before adding to the tall cup to avoid any heat damage to parts. Some people choose not to follow this recommendation and add the hot ingredients to the NUTRiBULLET and blend immediately for a ready-to-eat pasta sauce).

RED PEPPER PASTA SAUCE

350 calories per serving

Ingredients

- 1 red pepper, deseeded & sliced
- ½ onion, chopped
- 1 garlic clove, crushed
- 60ml/¼ cup vegetable stock
- ½ tsp brown sugar

- 75g/3oz dried pasta
- 1 tsp grated Parmesan cheese
- Low cal cooking oil spray
- Salt & pepper to taste

Method

1 In a frying pan gently sauté the sliced peppers, onion & garlic in a little low cal spray for about 10 minutes or until everything is nicely softened and combined. Add the stock & sugar and cook for a further two minutes. Remove from the heat, and leave to cool for a little while.

2 Meanwhile place the pasta in a pan of salted boiling water and cook until tender.

3 Now add the contents of the frying pan to the NUTRiBULLET tall cup. Be careful the ingredients don't go past the MAX line on your machine.

4 Twist on the NUTRiBULLET blade, turn the cup over and give it a tap down to make sure all the ingredients fall onto the blade. Attach to the NUTRiBULLET power base and pulse until smooth.

5 Scoop out the sauce and toss with the hot drained pasta in a hot pan. Alter the consistency by adding a little water if needed. Reheat, check the seasoning, sprinkle with Parmesan and serve.

CHEFS NOTE

Bags of sliced fresh peppers are available in most stores if you want to save on prep time.

(Please note: Per our method, the manufacturers of the NUTRiBULLET recommend you allow ingredients to cool before adding to the tall cup to avoid any heat damage to parts. Some people choose not to follow this recommendation and add the hot ingredients to the NUTRiBULLET and blend immediately for a ready-to-eat pasta sauce).

Skinny
RICE
COUSCOUS & NOODLES
MEALS IN MINUTES

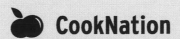 CookNation

NUOC CHAM CHICKEN & RICE

412 calories per serving

Ingredients

- ½ onion, chopped
- 125g/4oz precooked long grain rice (cooked weight)
- 100g/3½oz cooked chicken breast, shredded
- 2 garlic cloves

- 2 red chillies, deseeded
- 2 tbsp lime juice
- 2 tbsp fish sauce
- 2 tsp caster sugar
- Low cal cooking oil spray
- Salt & pepper to taste

Method

1 In a frying pan gently sauté the onion, rice and chicken in a little low cal spray for 5 minutes or until everything is cooked through and piping hot (add a little water to the pan if needed).

2 Meanwhile add the garlic, chilli, lime juice, fish sauce & caster sugar to the NUTRiBULLET short cup. Be careful the ingredients don't go past the MAX line on your machine.

3 Twist on the NUTRiBULLET blade, turn the cup over and give it a tap down to make sure all the ingredients fall onto the blade. Attach to the NUTRiBULLET power base and pulse until smooth.

4 This sauce is powerful! Serve it drizzled all over the rice and chicken for a massive taste bud blast.

CHEFS NOTE
Try precooking the rice in chicken stock for extra flavour.

CRAB NOODLE SALAD

449 calories per serving

Ingredients

- ½ red onion, finely sliced
- 150g/5oz precooked, cooled egg noodles (cooked weight)
- 125g/4oz cooked crab meat, shredded
- 1 bunch spring onions/scallions, chopped
- ¼ cucumber, finely chopped
- ½ red pepper, deseeded & sliced
- 2 garlic cloves

- 1 red chilli, deseeded
- 2 tbsp lime juice
- 1 stalk lemongrass
- 1 tsp caster sugar
- 2 tbsp water
- Salt & pepper to taste

Method

1 Gently toss together the onions, noodles, crab, spring onion, cucumber & pepper to make a noodle salad.

2 Meanwhile add the garlic, chilli, lime juice, lemongrass, sugar & water to the NUTRiBULLET short cup. Be careful the ingredients don't go past the MAX line on your machine.

3 Twist on the NUTRiBULLET blade, turn the cup over and give it a tap down to make sure all the ingredients fall onto the blade. Attach to the NUTRiBULLET power base and pulse until smooth. Check the balance of flavour, combine with the noodle salad and serve.

CHEFS NOTE

Dried noodles are really quick to cook and cool if you don't have precooked noodles to hand.

NASI GORENG

495 calories per serving

Ingredients

- 2 garlic cloves
- 1 red chilli, deseeded
- 2 tbsp soy sauce
- ½ onion
- 2 tsp caster sugar
- 75g/3oz peas
- 125g/4oz precooked long grain rice (cooked weight)

- 75g/3oz cooked chicken breast, shredded
- 1 egg
- 4 spring onions/scallions, chopped
- Low cal cooking oil spray
- Salt & pepper to taste

Method

1 Add the garlic, chilli, soy sauce, onion & caster sugar to the NUTRiBULLET short cup. Be careful the ingredients don't go past the MAX line on your machine.

2 Twist on the NUTRiBULLET blade, turn the cup over and give it a tap down to make sure all the ingredients fall onto the blade. Attach the short cup to the NUTRiBULLET power base and pulse until smooth.

3 In a frying pan gently sauté the mixture from the NUTRiBULLET & the peas in a little low cal spray for 5 minutes or until everything is nicely softened (add a little water to the pan if needed).

4 Add the rice, chicken and egg and stir-fry for a further 3-5 minutes or until everything is cooked through and piping hot. Serve with the chopped spring onions sprinkled over the top.

CHEFS NOTE

Try using prawns instead of chicken and add a little fish sauce.

CHICKEN COUSCOUS

499
calories per serving

Ingredients

- 50g/2oz couscous
- 100g/3½oz cooked chicken breast, shredded
- 2 tbsp lemon juice
- 1 tbsp balsamic vinegar

- 1 tbsp olive oil
- 1 tbsp fresh mint
- ½ cucumber
- 2 spring onions/scallions
- Salt & pepper to taste

Method

1 Prepare the couscous by adding approx. 80ml of boiling water or stock to a pan. Cover and leave to stand for 5 minutes.

2 Meanwhile add the lemon juice, vinegar, olive oil, mint, cucumber and spring onions to the NUTRiBULLET short cup. Be careful the ingredients don't go past the MAX line on your machine.

3 Twist on the NUTRiBULLET blade, turn the cup over and give it a tap down to make sure all the ingredients fall onto the blade. Attach to the NUTRiBULLET power base and pulse one second at a time until everything is finely chopped but not pureed.

4 Fluff the couscous with a fork, toss through the chunky dressing from the NUTRiBULLET and serve with the shredded chicken on top with lots of salt & freshly ground black pepper.

CHEFS NOTE

Try using flavoured couscous. There are lots of varieties available.

SALSA COUSCOUS

345 calories per serving

Ingredients

- 50g/2oz couscous
- 1 tbsp lemon juice
- 1 tbsp olive oil
- 125g/4oz cherry tomatoes
- 2 tbsp fresh coriander/cilantro
- 4 spring onions/scallions
- Salt & pepper to taste

Method

1 Prepare the couscous by adding approx. 80ml of boiling water or stock to a pan. Cover and leave to stand for 5 minutes.

2 Meanwhile add the lemon juice, olive oil, tomatoes, coriander and spring onions to the NUTRiBULLET short cup. Be careful the ingredients don't go past the MAX line on your machine.

3 Twist on the NUTRiBULLET blade, turn the cup over and give it a tap down to make sure all the ingredients fall onto the blade. Attach to the NUTRiBULLET power base and pulse one second at a time until everything is finely chopped but not pureed.

4 Fluff the couscous with a fork, toss through the salsa from the NUTRiBULLET and serve with plenty of salt & freshly ground black pepper.

CHEFS NOTE
Adjust the balance of flavours in the salsa to suit your own taste.

COUSCOUS TABBOULEH

260 calories per serving

Ingredients

- 50g/2oz couscous
- 1 vine ripened tomato
- ¼ cucumber
- Large bunch of flat leaf parsley
- 1 tbsp lemon juice
- ½ red onion
- 1 garlic clove, peeled
- Salt & pepper to taste

Method

1 Prepare the couscous by adding approx. 80ml of boiling water or stock to a pan. Cover and leave to stand for 5 minutes.

2 Meanwhile add the tomato, cucumber, parsley, lemon juice, red onion & garlic clove to the NUTRiBULLET short cup. Be careful the ingredients don't go past the MAX line on your machine.

3 Twist on the NUTRiBULLET blade, turn the cup over and give it a tap down to make sure all the ingredients fall onto the blade. Attach to the NUTRiBULLET power base and pulse one second at a time until everything is finely chopped but not pureed.

4 Fluff the couscous with a fork and toss through the herb & onion mixture from the NUTRiBULLET. Serve with plenty of salt & freshly ground black pepper.

CHEFS NOTE

This classic middle eastern dish is most often served with bulger wheat.

PEANUT NOODLES

390 calories per serving

Ingredients

- 150g/5oz precooked, cooled, egg noodles (cooked weight)
- 1 bunch spring onions/scallions, chopped
- ¼ cucumber
- 1 tbsp soy sauce

- 1 tbsp sweet chilli sauce
- 1 tbsp low fat peanut butter
- 1 tbsp lime juice
- Salt & pepper to taste

Method

1 Gently toss together noodles & spring onions to make a noodle salad.

2 Meanwhile add the cucumber, soy sauce, sweet chilli sauce, peanut butter & lime juice to the NUTRiBULLET short cup. Be careful the ingredients don't go past the MAX line on your machine.

3 Twist on the NUTRiBULLET blade, turn the cup over and give it a tap down to make sure all the ingredients fall onto the blade. Attach to the NUTRiBULLET power base and pulse a second at a time until the cucumber is finely chopped but not pureed.

4 Combine with the noodle salad and serve.

CHEFS NOTE
This is perfect for preparing in the morning and taking to work for a tasty lunch.

PAK CHOI NOODLES

446 calories per serving

Ingredients

- 1 garlic clove, peeled
- ½ red chilli, deseeded
- 2 tbsp soy sauce
- 2cm/1 inch piece fresh ginger
- 1 tsp sesame oil
- 1 tbsp lime juice
- ½ pak choi/bok choi, shredded
- ½ onion, finely sliced
- 150g/5oz precooked, or straight to wok egg noodles (cooked weight)
- 1 egg
- Salt & pepper to taste

Method

1 Add the garlic, chilli, soy sauce, ginger, sesame oil & lime juice to the NUTRiBULLET short cup. Be careful the ingredients don't go past the MAX line on your machine.

2 Twist on the NUTRiBULLET blade, turn the cup over and give it a tap down to make sure all the ingredients fall onto the blade. Attach to the NUTRiBULLET power base and pulse until smooth.

3 Meanwhile gently sauté the pak choi and onion in a little low cal spray for 5 minutes until softened (add a splash of water to the pan if needed).

4 Add the noodles and the dressing from the NUTRiBULLET. Continue to cook for 5 minutes until everything is well combined and piping hot. Make a 'well' in the noodles and break the egg into it. Cover and leave to gently cook for a few more minutes or until the egg is set & cooked to your liking.

5 Gently slide the noodles and egg into a shallow bowl and serve.

CHEFS NOTE

Don't worry if the egg breaks up when you are serving. Or just eat it straight out the pan!

THAI LAKSA

470 calories per serving

Ingredients

- 60ml/¼ cup chicken stock
- 75g/3oz cooked chicken breast, shredded
- 50g/2oz asparagus, chopped
- 150g/5oz precooked, or straight to wok egg noodles (cooked weight)
- 1 garlic clove, peeled
- ½ red chilli, deseeded
- 1 tsp turmeric
- 1 tbsp fish sauce
- 1 tbsp soy sauce
- 2cm/1 inch piece fresh ginger
- 120ml/½ cup low fat coconut milk
- Salt & pepper to taste

Method

1 Place the stock, chicken, asparagus & noodles in a saucepan on a medium heat.

2 Meanwhile add the garlic, chilli, turmeric, fish sauce, soy sauce, ginger & coconut milk to the NUTRiBULLET short cup. Be careful the ingredients don't go past the MAX line on your machine.

3 Twist on the NUTRiBULLET blade, turn the cup over and give it a tap down to make sure all the ingredients fall onto the blade. Attach to the NUTRiBULLET power base and pulse until smooth.

4 Add this to the noodles and cook for 2-3 minutes or until everything is piping hot and cooked through. Season well & serve in shallow bowls.

CHEFS NOTE
Adjust the coconut milk or stock if you want a more 'liquid' laksa.

Skinny
CHICKEN
MEALS IN MINUTES

 CookNation

CHICKEN BREAST WITH BASIL & TOMATO SAUCE

320 calories per serving

Ingredients

- 200g/7oz cherry tomatoes, halved
- ½ onion, chopped
- 1 garlic clove, crushed
- ½ tsp each of brown sugar & salt
- 2 tbsp tomato ketchup

- 2 tbsp chopped basil
- 125g/4oz skinless chicken breast
- 75g/3oz watercress
- Low cal cooking oil spray
- Salt & pepper to taste

Method

1 Preheat the grill to medium.

2 In a frying pan gently sauté the cherry tomatoes, onion, garlic, sugar, salt & ketchup in a little low cal spray for about 10-12 minutes or until everything is nicely softened and combined (add a little water to the pan if needed). Remove from the heat, and leave to cool for a little while.

3 Meanwhile cook the chicken breast under the grill for 8-11 minutes or until the chicken is cooked through.

4 Now add the contents of the frying pan to the NUTRiBULLET tall cup. Be careful the ingredients don't go past the MAX line on your machine.

5 Twist on the NUTRiBULLET blade, turn the cup over and give it a tap down to make sure all the ingredients fall onto the blade. Attach to the NUTRiBULLET power base and pulse until smooth.

6 Scoop out the sauce and add to a hot pan. Alter the consistency by adding a little water if needed. Reheat, check the seasoning and serve poured over the chicken breast with the watercress on the side of the plate.

(Please note: Per our method, the manufacturers of the NUTRiBULLET recommend you allow ingredients to cool before adding to the tall cup to avoid any heat damage to parts. Some people choose not to follow this recommendation and add the hot ingredients to the NUTRiBULLET and blend immediately for a ready-to-eat sauce).

CHICKEN BREAST WITH GARLIC & ZUCCHINI SAUCE

365 calories per serving

Ingredients

- 1 large courgette, sliced
- ½ onion, chopped
- 2 garlic cloves, crushed
- 60ml/¼ cup chicken stock
- 125g/4oz skinless chicken breast
- 50g/2oz spinach
- 1 tsp olive oil
- Salt & pepper to taste

Method

1 Preheat the grill to medium.

2 In a frying pan gently sauté the courgette, onion & garlic in the olive oil for 5 minutes. Add the stock and cook for a further 5-8 minutes or until everything is nicely softened and combined. Remove from the heat, and leave to cool for a little while.

3 Meanwhile cook the chicken breast under the grill for 8-11 minutes or until the chicken is cooked through.

4 Now add the contents of the frying pan to the NUTRiBULLET tall cup. Be careful the ingredients don't go past the MAX line on your machine.

5 Twist on the NUTRiBULLET blade, turn the cup over and give it a tap down to make sure all the ingredients fall onto the blade. Attach to the NUTRiBULLET power base and pulse until smooth.

6 Scoop out the sauce and add to a hot pan. Alter the consistency by adding a little water if needed. Reheat and check the seasoning.

7 Add the spinach to the empty frying on a medium heat and wilt for a minute or two.

8 Serve the courgette sauce poured over the hot chicken breast with the wilted spinach on the side.

(Please note: Per our method, the manufacturers of the NUTRiBULLET recommend you allow ingredients to cool before adding to the tall cup to avoid any heat damage to parts. Some people choose not to follow this recommendation and add the hot ingredients to the NUTRiBULLET and blend immediately for a ready-to-eat sauce).

PINEAPPLE SALSA OVER CHICKEN

468 calories per serving

Ingredients

- 100g/3½oz tinned pineapple
- Small bunch of coriander
- Small bunch of spring onions/scallions
- 1 tbsp lime juice
- 125g/4oz skinless chicken breast
- 50g/5oz couscous
- Salt & pepper to taste

REFRESHING!

Method

1 Preheat the grill to medium and cook the chicken breast for 8-11 minutes or until the chicken is cooked through.

2 Prepare the couscous by adding approx. 80ml of boiling water or stock to a pan. Cover and leave to stand for 5 minutes.

3 Add the pineapple, coriander, spring onions & lime juice to the NUTRiBULLET tall cup. Be careful the ingredients don't go past the MAX line on your machine.

4 Twist on the NUTRiBULLET blade, turn the cup over and give it a tap down to make sure all the

ingredients fall onto the blade. Attach to the NUTRiBULLET power base and pulse for one second at a time. You want to end up with a textured salsa not a puree.

5 Fluff up the couscous with a fork. Scoop out the sauce and serve piled over the hot chicken breast with the couscous on the side.

CHEFS NOTE

You could serve this as a cold lunch served over thick slices of cold precooked chicken.

CHICKEN BREAST WITH MUSHROOM & CRÈME FRAICHE

365 calories per serving

Ingredients

- 125g/4oz chestnut mushrooms
- ½ onion or 2 shallots, chopped
- 1 garlic clove, crushed
- 2 tbsp low fat crème fraiche or low fat cream
- 1 tsp Dijon mustard
- 125g/4oz skinless chicken breast
- 50g/2oz Rocket
- 1 tsp olive oil
- Salt & pepper to taste

Method

1 Preheat the grill to medium.

2 In a frying pan gently sauté the mushrooms, onion & garlic in the olive oil for 8-10 minutes or until everything is nicely softened and combined. Stir through the mustard and crème fraiche for a minute or two. Remove from the heat, and leave to cool for a little while.

3 Meanwhile cook the chicken breast under the grill for 8-11 minutes or until the chicken is cooked through.

4 Now add the contents of the frying pan to the NUTRiBULLET tall cup. Be careful the ingredients don't go past the MAX line on your machine.

5 Twist on the NUTRiBULLET blade, turn the cup over and give it a tap down to make sure all the ingredients fall onto the blade. Attach to the NUTRiBULLET power base and pulse until smooth.

6 Scoop out the sauce and add to a hot pan. Alter the consistency by adding a little water if needed. Reheat and check the seasoning.

7 Serve the mushroom sauce poured over the hot chicken breast with the rocket on the side.

CHEFS NOTE

Use English mustard for a stronger taste.

(Please note: Per our method, the manufacturers of the NUTRiBULLET recommend you allow ingredients to cool before adding to the tall cup to avoid any heat damage to parts. Some people choose not to follow this recommendation and add the hot ingredients to the NUTRiBULLET and blend immediately for a ready-to-eat sauce).

CHICKEN BREAST WITH MASALA SAUCE

480 calories per serving

Ingredients

- ½ onion
- 1 garlic clove, crushed
- ½ tsp each garam masala, turmeric, ginger & chilli powder
- 1 tsp ground almonds
- 100g/3½oz tinned tomatoes

- 2 tbsp low fat cream
- 125g/4oz skinless chicken breast
- 50g/2oz microwaveable rice
- Low cal cooking oil spray
- Salt & pepper to taste

Method

1 Preheat the grill to medium.

2 In a frying pan gently sauté the onion & garlic in a little low cal spray for 5 minutes. Add the dried spices, almonds & tomatoes and cook for 4-6 minutes or until everything is nicely softened and combined (add a little water to the pan if needed).

3 Remove from the heat, and leave to cool for a little while.

4 Meanwhile cook the chicken breast under the grill for 8-11 minutes or until the chicken is cooked through.

5 Add the contents of the frying pan to the NUTRiBULLET tall cup. Be careful the ingredients don't go past the MAX line on your machine.

6 Twist on the NUTRiBULLET blade, turn the cup over and give it a tap down to make sure all the ingredients fall onto the blade. Attach to the NUTRiBULLET power base and pulse until smooth.

7 Scoop out the sauce and add to a hot pan. Alter the consistency by adding a little water if needed. Reheat, check the seasoning and stir through the cream.

8 Heat the rice according to manufacturers instructions. Serve the masala sauce poured over the hot chicken breast with the rice on the side.

(Please note: Per our method, the manufacturers of the NUTRiBULLET recommend you allow ingredients to cool before adding to the tall cup to avoid any heat damage to parts. Some people choose not to follow this recommendation and add the hot ingredients to the NUTRiBULLET and blend immediately for a ready-to-eat sauce).

HONEY & MUSTARD POUR OVER SAUCE

490
calories per serving

Ingredients

- 1 onion, chopped
- ½ carrot, finely sliced
- 1 garlic clove, crushed
- 2 tbsp dry cider
- 1 tsp wholegrain mustard
- 1 tsp honey
- 2 tbsp low fat cream

- 125g/4oz skinless chicken breast
- 1 tsp olive oil
- 100g/3½oz chickpeas
- Large handful of rocket
- 1 tsp lemon juice
- Salt & pepper to taste

Method

1 Preheat the grill to medium.

2 In a frying pan gently sauté the onions, carrots & garlic in the olive oil for 8-10 minutes or until everything is nicely softened and combined. Stir through the cider, mustard and honey. Remove from the heat, and leave to cool for a little while.

3 Meanwhile cook the chicken breast under the grill for 8-11 minutes or until the chicken is cooked through.

4 Now add the contents of the frying pan to the NUTRiBULLET tall cup. Be careful the ingredients don't go past the MAX line on your machine.

5 Twist on the NUTRiBULLET blade, turn the cup over and give it a tap down to make sure all the ingredients fall onto the blade. Attach to the NUTRiBULLET power base and pulse until smooth.

6 Scoop out the sauce and add to a hot pan. Alter the consistency by adding a little water if needed. Reheat and check the seasoning.

7 Toss the rocket, chickpeas and lemon juice together with plenty of salt and pepper

8 Stir the cream through the mustard sauce and serve poured over the hot chicken breast with the chickpea and rocket salad on the side of the plate.

(Please note: Per our method, the manufacturers of the NUTRiBULLET recommend you allow ingredients to cool before adding to the tall cup to avoid any heat damage to parts. Some people choose not to follow this recommendation and add the hot ingredients to the NUTRiBULLET and blend immediately for a ready-to-eat sauce).

Skinny
SEAFOOD
MEALS IN MINUTES

GRILLED COD WITH PEA PUREE

260 calories per serving

Ingredients

- 150g/5oz boneless cod loin
- 125g/4oz frozen peas
- 1 tbsp fresh chopped mint
- 1 tbsp lemon juice
- 2 tbsp low fat cream
- 50g/5oz watercress
- Low cal cooking oil spray
- Salt & pepper to taste

Method

1 Preheat the grill to medium and cook the cod loin for 6-9 minutes (turning once) or until cooked through.

2 In a saucepan place the peas in boiling water and cook for 3-4 minutes, put to one side and cool for a few minutes.

3 Now add the peas, mint, lemon juice & cream to the NUTRiBULLET tall cup. Be careful the ingredients don't go past the MAX line on your machine.

4 Twist on the NUTRiBULLET blade, turn the cup over and give it a tap down to make sure all the ingredients fall onto the blade. Attach to the NUTRiBULLET power base and pulse until smooth.

5 Scoop out the sauce and place in a warm pan. Alter the consistency by adding a little water if needed. Carefully reheat, check the seasoning and serve on top of the hot cod with the watercress on the side.

CHEFS NOTE

Pulse rather than purée the peas if you want a coarser texture.

(Please note: Per our method, the manufacturers of the NUTRiBULLET recommend you allow ingredients to cool before adding to the tall cup to avoid any heat damage to parts. Some people choose not to follow this recommendation and add the hot ingredients to the NUTRiBULLET and blend immediately for a ready-to-eat sauce).

PEANUT & COCONUT MILK FISH PESTO

295 calories per serving

Ingredients

- 150g/5oz boneless cod loin
- 1 small bunch of coriander/cilantro
- 1 medium tomato
- ½ garlic clove, peeled
- 2cm/1 inch piece peeled fresh ginger
- 1 tbsp peanuts
- 1 tsp fish sauce
- 60ml/¼ cup low fat coconut milk
- 75g/3oz spring greens
- Lime wedges to serve
- Salt & pepper to taste

Method

1 Preheat the grill to medium and cook the cod loin for 6-9 minutes (turning once) or until cooked through.

2 Meanwhile plunge the spring greens in salted boiling water and cook for 2-3 minutes, or until tender.

3 Add the coriander, tomato, garlic, ginger, peanuts, fish sauce & coconut milk to the NUTRiBULLET tall cup. Be careful the ingredients don't go past the MAX line on your machine.

4 Twist on the NUTRiBULLET blade, turn the cup over and give it a tap down to make sure all the ingredients fall onto the blade. Attach to the NUTRiBULLET power base and pulse until smooth.

5 Scoop out the sauce and serve on top of the hot cod with the drained spring greens and lime wedges on the side of the plate.

CHEFS NOTE
Try dressing the spring greens with a little garlic oil.

PARSLEY & WALNUT FISH PESTO SAUCE

245 calories per serving

Ingredients

- 150g/5oz boneless haddock fillet
- 1 small bunch of flat leaf parsley
- ½ garlic clove, peeled
- 1 tbsp shelled walnuts
- 1 tsp grated Parmesan cheese
- 2 tbsp olive oil
- 50g/5oz rocket
- Salt & pepper to taste

NUTTY!

Method

1 Preheat the grill to medium and cook the haddock fillet for 6-9 minutes (turning once) or until cooked through.

2 Add the parsley, garlic, walnuts, cheese & oil to the NUTRiBULLET tall cup. Be careful the ingredients don't go past the MAX line on your machine.

3 Twist on the NUTRiBULLET blade, turn the cup over and give it a tap down to make sure all the ingredients fall onto the blade. Attach to the NUTRiBULLET power base and pulse until smooth (add a little water if needed to loosen up the pesto).

4 Scoop out the sauce and serve on top of the hot fish fillet with the rocket on the side.

CHEFS NOTE

Use any firm white fish you like with this pesto.

SEA BASS & BALSAMIC TOMATO SAUCE

395 calories per serving

Ingredients

- 175g/6oz thick sea bass fillet
- ½ onion
- 1 tbsp balsamic vinegar
- 125g/4oz cherry tomatoes, halved
- 1 garlic clove, crushed
- 1 tbsp tomato puree/paste
- 125g/4oz tenderstem broccoli
- Low cal cooking oil spray
- Salt & pepper to taste

Method

1 Preheat the grill to medium.

2 In a frying pan gently sauté the onion, balsamic vinegar, tomatoes, garlic & puree in a little low cal spray for about 10-12 minutes or until everything is nicely softened and combined. Remove from the heat, and leave to cool for a little while.

3 Meanwhile cook the sea bass under the grill for 8-11 minutes (turning once) or until cooked through.

4 Now add the contents of the frying pan to the NUTRiBULLET tall cup. Be careful the ingredients don't go past the MAX line on your machine.

5 Twist on the NUTRiBULLET blade, turn the cup over and give it a tap down to make sure all the ingredients fall onto the blade. Attach to the NUTRiBULLET power base and pulse until smooth.

6 Plunge the broccoli into a pan of salted boiling water and cook for 2-3 minutes or until tender.

7 Scoop out the sauce and add to a hot pan. Alter the consistency by adding a little water if needed. Reheat, check the seasoning and serve poured over the hot sea bass fillet with the broccoli on the side.

(Please note: Per our method, the manufacturers of the NUTRiBULLET recommend you allow ingredients to cool before adding to the tall cup to avoid any heat damage to parts. Some people choose not to follow this recommendation and add the hot ingredients to the NUTRiBULLET and blend immediately for a ready-to-eat sauce).

Skinny
MEALS IN MINUTES
FRITTATAS

···

The NUTRiBULLET improves the texture of omelettes & frittatas by forcing air into the mixture and making them light and fluffy.

···

 CookNation

PEPPER & SPINACH FRITTATA

SERVES 1

350 calories per serving

Ingredients

- 4 eggs
- 1 roasted red pepper (out of a jar)
- 2 handfuls of spinach
- ½ garlic clove, peeled
- Big pinch of salt
- 1 tsp low fat olive 'butter' spread
- Salt & pepper to taste

USE FREE RANGE EGGS

Method

1 Add all the ingredients, except the 'butter', to the NUTRiBULLET tall cup. Be careful the ingredients don't go past the MAX line on your machine.

2 Twist on the NUTRiBULLET blade, turn the cup over and give it a tap down to make sure all the ingredients fall onto the blade. Attach to the NUTRiBULLET power base and pulse until the vegetables are finely chopped, but not pureed.

3 On a gentle heat melt the low fat 'butter' spread in a small non-stick frying pan. Give the cup a good shake and pour in the egg mixture. Cover and leave to cook for 8-10 minutes or until the eggs are set.

4 Finish the frittata under a hot grill for a couple of minutes if you want it nicely browned.

5 Slide onto a plate, cut into wedges, season & serve.

CHEFS NOTE
Add half a red chilli if you want a 'kick'.

52

SPRING ONION & FETA FRITTATA

420 calories per serving

Ingredients

TRY RICOTTA CHEESE

- 4 eggs
- 4 spring onions/scallions
- 50g/2oz asparagus tips
- 50g/2oz low fat feta cheese
- 2 tbsp milk
- Big pinch of salt
- 1 tsp low fat olive 'butter' spread
- Salt & pepper to taste

Method

1 Add all the ingredients, except the 'butter', to the NUTRiBULLET tall cup. Be careful the ingredients don't go past the MAX line on your machine.

2 Twist on the NUTRiBULLET blade, turn the cup over and give it a tap down to make sure all the ingredients fall onto the blade. Attach to the NUTRiBULLET power base and pulse until the vegetables are finely chopped, but not pureed.

3 On a gentle heat melt the low fat 'butter' spread in a small non-stick frying pan. Give the cup a good shake and pour in the egg mixture. Cover and leave to cook for 8-10 minutes or until the eggs are set.

4 Finish the frittata under a hot grill for a couple of minutes if you want it nicely browned.

5 Slide onto a plate, cut into wedges, season & serve.

CHEFS NOTE
You could use a shallots instead of spring onions.

SPANISH OMELETTE

490
calories per
serving

Ingredients

- 4 eggs
- 4 spring onions/scallions
- 50g/2oz sliced chorizo sausage
- Large bunch of flat leaf parsley
- Big pinch of salt
- 1 tsp low fat olive 'butter' spread
- Salt & pepper to taste

Method

1 Add all the ingredients, except the 'butter', to the NUTRiBULLET tall cup. Be careful the ingredients don't go past the MAX line on your machine.

2 Twist on the NUTRiBULLET blade, turn the cup over and give it a tap down to make sure all the ingredients fall onto the blade. Attach the tall cup to the NUTRiBULLET power base and pulse until the chorizo and parsley is finely chopped, but not pureed.

3 On a gentle heat melt the low fat 'butter' spread in a small non-stick frying pan. Give the cup a good shake and pour in the egg mixture. Cover and leave to cook for 8-10 minutes or until the eggs are set.

4 Finish the omelette under a hot grill for a couple of minutes if you want it nicely browned.

5 Slide onto a plate, cut into wedges, season with lots of black pepper & serve.

CHEFS NOTE

Try adding a teaspoon of paprika.

CHEESE & CHERRY TOMATO FRITTATA

400 calories per serving

Ingredients

- 4 eggs
- ½ garlic clove, peeled
- 50g/2oz low fat grated cheddar cheese
- Large pinch of salt
- 6 cherry tomatoes, halved
- 1 tsp low fat olive 'butter' spread
- Salt & pepper to taste

ADD FRESH BASIL

Method

1 Add all the ingredients, except the 'butter' & cherry tomatoes, to the NUTRiBULLET tall cup. Be careful the ingredients don't go past the MAX line on your machine.

2 Twist on the NUTRiBULLET blade, turn the cup over and give it a tap down to make sure all the ingredients fall onto the blade. Attach to the NUTRiBULLET power base and pulse for a few seconds to chop the garlic.

3 On a gentle heat melt the low fat 'butter' spread in a small non-stick frying pan. Add the cherry tomatoes to the cup but don't pulse. Give it a good shake and pour the egg mixture into the pan.

Cover and leave to cook for 10-12 minutes or until the eggs are set and the tomatoes are tender.

4 Finish the frittata under a hot grill for a couple of minutes if you want it nicely browned.

5 Slide onto a plate, cut into wedges, season & serve.

MUSHROOM FRITTATA

360
calories per serving

Ingredients

- 4 eggs
- 75g/3oz mushrooms
- 1 tsp Dijon mustard
- ½ tsp turmeric
- ½ garlic clove, peeled
- Large pinch of salt
- 1 tsp low fat olive 'butter' spread
- Salt & pepper to taste

TRY PORCINI MUSHROOMS

Method

1 Add all the ingredients, except the 'butter', to the NUTRiBULLET tall cup. Be careful the ingredients don't go past the MAX line on your machine.

2 Twist on the NUTRiBULLET blade, turn the cup over and give it a tap down to make sure all the ingredients fall onto the blade. Attach the tall cup to the NUTRiBULLET power base and pulse until the mushrooms are finely chopped, but not pureed.

3 On a gentle heat melt the low fat 'butter' spread in a small non-stick frying pan. Give the cup a good shake and pour in the egg mixture. Cover and leave to cook for 8-10 minutes or until the eggs are set.

4 Finish the frittata under a hot grill for a couple of minutes if you want it nicely browned.

5 Slide onto a plate, cut into wedges, season & serve.

FRESH HERB & RICOTTA FRITTATA

380 calories per serving

Ingredients

- 4 eggs
- 1 handful of spinach
- 50g/2oz low fat ricotta cheese
- 2 tbsp milk
- Small bunch of chives

- Small bunch of fresh parsley or basil
- 1 garlic clove, peeled
- Large pinch of salt
- 1 tsp low fat olive 'butter' spread
- Salt & pepper to taste

Method

1 Add all the ingredients, except the 'butter', to the NUTRiBULLET tall cup. Be careful the ingredients don't go past the MAX line on your machine.

2 Twist on the NUTRiBULLET blade, turn the cup over and give it a tap down to make sure all the ingredients fall onto the blade. Attach to the NUTRiBULLET power base and pulse until the spinach & herbs are finely chopped, but not pureed.

3 On a gentle heat melt the low fat 'butter' spread in a small non-stick frying pan. Give the cup a good shake and pour in the egg mixture. Cover and leave to cook for 8-10 minutes or until the eggs are set.

4 Finish the frittata under a hot grill for a couple of minutes if you want it nicely browned.

5 Slide onto a plate, cut into wedges, season & serve.

CHEFS NOTE

Use any mix of fresh herbs you prefer for this frittata.

SPRING GREEN & BASIL OMELETTE

SERVES 1

360 calories per serving

Ingredients

- 50g/2oz spring greens
- 4 eggs
- 2 spring onions/scallions
- Small bunch of basil
- Large pinch of salt
- 1 tsp low fat olive 'butter' spread
- Salt & pepper to taste

 TRY USING KALE

Method

1 Plunge the spring greens into a pan of salted boiling water and cook for 1 minute before draining.

2 Add all the ingredients, except the 'butter', to the NUTRiBULLET tall cup. Be careful the ingredients don't go past the MAX line on your machine.

3 Twist on the NUTRiBULLET blade, turn the cup over and give it a tap down to make sure all the ingredients fall onto the blade. Attach to the NUTRiBULLET power base and pulse until the greens & onions are finely chopped, but not pureed.

4 On a gentle heat melt the low fat 'butter' spread in a small non-stick frying pan. Give the cup a good shake and pour in the egg mixture. Cover and leave to cook for 8-10 minutes or until the eggs are set.

5 Finish the frittata under a hot grill for a couple of minutes if you want it nicely browned.

6 Slide onto a plate, cut into wedges, season & serve.

Skinny
MEALS IN MINUTES
PANCAKES

Pancakes aren't just for breakfast! Experiment with toppings and ingredients to perfect your ideal superfast supper. All recipes make one single pancake cooked in a 19cm/5½inch pan. Feel free to double or triple the quantities if you are hungry or cooking for others.

BANANA PANCAKES

185 calories per serving

Ingredients

- **1 banana, peeled**
- **1 egg**
- **½ tsp baking powder**
- **½ tsp vanilla extract**
- **1 tsp low fat olive 'butter' spread**

Method

1 Add the banana, egg, baking powder & vanilla extract to the NUTRiBULLET short cup. Be careful the ingredients don't go past the MAX line on your machine.

2 Twist on the NUTRiBULLET blade, turn the cup over and give it a tap down to make sure all the ingredients fall onto the blade. Attach to the NUTRiBULLET power base and pulse until smooth.

3 On a gentle heat melt the low fat olive 'butter' spread in a small non-stick frying pan. Pour in the pancake batter and gently cook for about 4 minutes or until cooked through (turn once). Because of the banana this pancake takes longer to cook than an ordinary pancake so don't try to flip it too soon

CHEFS NOTE

Try adding a pinch of cinnamon or nutmeg to the pancake batter.

HONEY OAT PANCAKES

150 calories per serving

Ingredients

- 2 tbsp oats
- 1 egg
- 1 tsp honey
- ½ tsp vanilla extract
- 1 tsp low fat olive 'butter' spread

ADD BLUEBERRES!

Method

1 Add the oats, egg, honey & vanilla extract to the NUTRiBULLET short cup. Be careful the ingredients don't go past the MAX line on your machine.

2 Twist on the NUTRiBULLET blade, turn the cup over and give it a tap down to make sure all the ingredients fall onto the blade. Attach to the NUTRiBULLET power base and pulse until smooth.

3 On a gentle heat melt the low fat olive 'butter' spread in a small non-stick frying pan. Pour in the pancake batter and gently cook for about 1-2 minutes or until cooked through (turn once).

CHEFS NOTE
Try serving with a dollop of fat free Greek yoghurt.

FLAX SEED & SYRUP PANCAKES

SERVES 1

220 calories per serving

Ingredients

- 2 tbsp flax seeds
- 1 egg
- ½ tsp baking powder
- 1 tbsp milk
- 1 tsp low fat olive 'butter' spread
- 1 tbsp maple syrup

TRY HEMP SEEDS

Method

1 Add the flax seeds, egg, baking powder & milk to the NUTRiBULLET short cup. Be careful the ingredients don't go past the MAX line on your machine.

2 Twist on the NUTRiBULLET blade, turn the cup over and give it a tap down to make sure all the ingredients fall onto the blade. Attach to the NUTRiBULLET power base and pulse until smooth.

3 On a gentle heat melt the low fat olive 'butter' spread in a small non-stick frying pan. Pour in the pancake batter and gently cook for about 1-2 minutes or until cooked through (turn once). Serve with the maple syrup drizzled on top.

CHEFS NOTE

Flax seeds are packed with goodness, which will add a 'nutriboost' to your day.

62

STRAIGHT-UP SIMPLE PANCAKES

160 calories per serving

Ingredients

- 1 tbsp plain/all purpose flour
- 1 egg
- 60mL/¼ cup milk
- 1 tsp caster sugar
- 1 tsp low fat olive 'butter' spread

Method

1 Add the flour, egg, milk & caster sugar to the NUTRiBULLET short cup. Be careful the ingredients don't go past the MAX line on your machine.

2 Twist on the NUTRiBULLET blade, turn the cup over and give it a tap down to make sure all the ingredients fall onto the blade. Attach to the NUTRiBULLET power base and pulse until smooth.

3 On a gentle heat melt the low fat olive 'butter' spread in a small non-stick frying pan. Pour in the pancake batter and gently cook for about 1-2 minutes or until cooked through (turn once).

CHEFS NOTE
Serve with lemon juice and a sprinkle more sugar.

SPINACH PANCAKES

170 calories per serving

Ingredients

- 1 tbsp plain/all purpose flour
- 1 egg
- 60ml/¼ cup milk
- 1 small handful of spinach
- 1 tsp honey
- 1 tsp low fat olive 'butter' spread

Method

1 Add the flour, egg, milk, spinach & honey to the NUTRiBULLET short cup. Be careful the ingredients don't go past the MAX line on your machine.

2 Twist on the NUTRiBULLET blade, turn the cup over and give it a tap down to make sure all the ingredients fall onto the blade. Attach to the NUTRiBULLET power base and pulse until smooth.

3 On a gentle heat melt the low fat olive 'butter' spread in a small non-stick frying pan. Pour in the pancake batter and gently cook for about 1-2 minutes or until cooked through (turn once).

CHEFS NOTE

These iron rich pancakes are good with Greek yogurt.

CARROT & CORIANDER PANCAKES

180 calories per serving

Ingredients

GOOD WITH SOUP!

- 1 tbsp plain/all purpose flour
- 1 egg
- 60ml/¼ cup milk
- ½ carrot, sliced
- ½ tsp ground coriander/cilantro
- Pinch of salt
- 1 tsp low fat olive 'butter' spread

Method

1 Add the flour, egg, milk, carrot, coriander & salt to the NUTRiBULLET short cup. Be careful the ingredients don't go past the MAX line on your machine.

2 Twist on the NUTRiBULLET blade, turn the cup over and give it a tap down to make sure all the ingredients fall onto the blade. Attach to the NUTRiBULLET power base and pulse until smooth.

3 On a gentle heat melt the 'low fat olive 'butter' spread in a small non-stick frying pan. Pour in the pancake batter and gently cook for about 2-3 minutes or until cooked through (turn once).

CHEFS NOTE
Try serving these pancakes with a simple tomato salsa.

Skinny
MEALS IN MINUTES
DIPS

These dips are great for quick & easy snacks or light lunches. Feel free to increase the quantities if you wish. Each dip has a serving suggestion of crackers or pitta bread etc but these can be altered to suit your taste.

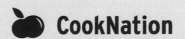 CookNation

FRESH PEA & MINT DIP

165 calories per serving

Ingredients

- 2 tsp fat free Greek yogurt
- 1 tsp freshly chopped mint
- 75g/3oz fresh peas
- 1 tsp grated Parmesan cheese
- 2 regular cream crackers

Method

1 Add all the ingredients, except the cream crackers, to the NUTRiBULLET short cup. Be careful the ingredients don't go past the MAX line on your machine.

2 Twist on the NUTRiBULLET blade, turn the cup over and give it tap a down to make sure all the ingredients fall onto the blade. Attach to the NUTRiBULLET power base and pulse for one second at a time to give you a textured dip. Don't blend for too long, as you don't want to end up with a smooth puree.

3 Scoop out the dip from the cup and serve loaded onto the cream crackers with plenty of salt and pepper.

CHEFS NOTE
Frozen peas are fine to use once they thaw.

SWEETCORN & CHERRY TOMATO TOPPER

185 calories per serving

Ingredients

- 75g/3oz tinned sweetcorn, drained
- 2 cherry tomatoes, halved
- 1 spring onion/scallion, chopped
- 1 tsp low fat mayonnaise
- 5 regular water biscuits

Method

1 Add all the ingredients, except the water biscuits, to the NUTRiBULLET short cup. Be careful the ingredients don't go past the MAX line on your machine.

2 Twist on the NUTRiBULLET blade, turn the cup over and give it a tap down to make sure all the ingredients fall onto the blade. Attach to the NUTRiBULLET power base and pulse for one second at a time to give you a textured dip. Don't blend for too long, as you don't want to end up with a smooth puree.

3 Scoop out the dip from the cup and spoon onto the water biscuits. Serve straight away.

CHEFS NOTE
Add a pinch of salt & some freshly ground black pepper.

SIMPLE TAPENADE

167
calories per
serving

Ingredients

- 75g/3oz pitted olives
- ½ tsp capers
- ½ garlic clove, peeled
- ½ red chilli, deseeded

- 1 tsp tomato puree/paste
- 1 tsp olive oil
- 2 wholegrain crackerbread

Method

1 Add all the ingredients, except the crackerbread, to the NUTRiBULLET short cup. Be careful the ingredients don't go past the MAX line on your machine.

2 Twist on the NUTRiBULLET blade, turn the cup over and give it a tap down to make sure all the ingredients fall onto the blade. Attach to the NUTRiBULLET power base and pulse for one second at a time to give you a textured/chopped dip. Don't blend for too long, as you don't want to end up with a smooth puree.

3 Scoop out the dip from the cup and spoon onto the crackerbread with plenty of salt & pepper.

CHEFS NOTE
Use green or olives for this tapenade. You could also add a teaspoon of anchovy paste if you have it.

BEANS & BREADSTICKS

198 calories per serving

Ingredients

- 75g/3oz tinned haricot beans, drained
- 1 tsp fresh mint or coriander/cilantro
- 50g/2oz low fat ricotta cheese
- 1 tsp olive oil
- 3 regular breadsticks

TRY FETA CHEESE

Method

1 Add all the ingredients, except the breadsticks, to the NUTRiBULLET short cup. Be careful the ingredients don't go past the MAX line on your machine.

2 Twist on the NUTRiBULLET blade, turn the cup over and give it tap a down to make sure all the ingredients fall onto the blade. Attach to the NUTRiBULLET power base and pulse for one second at a time to give you a textured dip. Don't blend for too long, as you don't want to end up with a smooth puree.

3 Scoop out the dip from the cup and put in a little dish. Season well and serve with the breadsticks.

CHEFS NOTE
Add a pinch of dried herbs if you don't have any fresh herbs to hand.

GREEK CREAM CHEESE PITTA

155 calories per serving

Ingredients

USE WHOLEMEAL PITTA

- 50g/2oz low fat cream cheese
- 1 tsp fat free Greek yogurt
- 2 tsp fresh chives
- ¼ cucumber
- 1 mini pitta bread

Method

1 Add all the ingredients, except the pitta bread, to the NUTRiBULLET short cup. Be careful the ingredients don't go past the MAX line on your machine.

2 Twist on the NUTRiBULLET blade, turn the cup over and give it tap a down to make sure all the ingredients fall onto the blade. Attach to the NUTRiBULLET power base and pulse for one second at a time to give you a textured dip. Don't blend for too long, as you don't want the cucumber to end up pureed.

3 Slice the pitta bread lengthways from top to bottom to open out and separate, so that you end up with two flat-breads. Scoop out the dip from the cup and spread over the two pitta halves. Eat as an open sandwich.

CHEFS NOTE
Make it simple by using cream cheese with the chives already added.

AVOCADO & CHORIZO

257 calories per serving

Ingredients

- ¼ ripe avocado
- 1 tsp lime juice
- 1 cherry tomato, halved
- 25g/1oz chorizo sausage, sliced
- 1 slice wholemeal bread

Method

1 Add all the ingredients, except the bread, to the NUTRiBULLET short cup. Be careful the ingredients don't go past the MAX line on your machine.

2 Twist on the NUTRiBULLET blade, turn the cup over and give it tap a down to make sure all the ingredients fall onto the blade. Attach to the NUTRiBULLET power base and pulse for one second at a time to give you a textured dip. Don't blend for too long, as you don't want the cucumber to end up pureed.

3 Lightly toast the bread and leave to cool. Scoop out the dip from the cup and spread over the toasted bread.

CHEFS NOTE
Use cooked chorizo deli sausage.

CORIANDER SALSA

203 calories per serving

Ingredients

- 2 vine-ripened tomatoes
- ½ red onion
- ½ red chilli, deseeded
- 2 tbsp fresh coriander/cilantro
- 1 tsp lemon juice
- 25g/1oz lightly salted tortilla chips

Method

1 Add all the ingredients, except the tortilla chips, to the NUTRiBULLET short cup. Be careful the ingredients don't go past the MAX line on your machine.

2 Twist on the NUTRiBULLET blade, turn the cup over and give it tap a down to make sure all the ingredients fall onto the blade. Attach to the NUTRiBULLET power base and pulse for one second at a time to give you a textured dip. Don't blend for too long, as you want things to be roughly chopped not pureed.

3 Scoop out the dip from the cup and put in a little dish. Season well and serve with the tortilla chips.

CHEFS NOTE
Balance the chilli, coriander and lemon juice to suit your own taste.

TZATZIKI & CRUDITES

135 calories per serving

Ingredients

- ½ cucumber
- 2 tbsp fat free Greek yogurt
- ½ garlic clove, peeled
- 1 tsp fresh mint

- 1 tsp olive oil
- 1 carrot, peeled & cut into batons
- ½ red pepper deseeded & sliced

Method

1 Add all the ingredients, except the carrot & pepper, to the NUTRiBULLET short cup. Be careful the ingredients don't go past the MAX line on your machine.

2 Twist on the NUTRiBULLET blade, turn the cup over and give it tap a down to make sure all the ingredients fall onto the blade. Attach to the NUTRiBULLET power base and pulse for one second at a time to give you a textured dip. Don't blend for too long, as you want the cucumber to be roughly chopped not pureed.

3 Scoop out the dip from the cup and put in a little dish. Season well and serve with the carrot batons & pepper slices.

CHEFS NOTE
Super quick tip: buy bags of pre-prepared carrots and pepper slices.

ARTICHOKE DIP

SERVES 1

145 calories per serving

Ingredients

- 100g/3½oz tinned artichokes, drained
- 2 tsp low fat mayonnaise
- ½ garlic clove, peeled
- 1 spring onion/scallion
- 5 regular water biscuits

SEASON WELL

Method

1 Add all the ingredients, except the water biscuits, to the NUTRiBULLET short cup. Be careful the ingredients don't go past the MAX line on your machine.

2 Twist on the NUTRiBULLET blade, turn the cup over and give it tap a down to make sure all the ingredients fall onto the blade. Attach to the NUTRiBULLET power base and pulse for one second at a time to give you a textured dip. Don't blend for too long, as you do not want to end up with a puree.

3 Scoop out the dip from the cup and serve loaded onto the water biscuits.

CHEFS NOTE
Artichokes can aid digestion and help reduce cholesterol levels.

SALMON RILLETTES

158
calories per
serving

Ingredients

- 75g/3oz precooked salmon fillet
- 1 tbsp fat free Greek yogurt
- 1 tsp lemon juice
- 1 tsp chives
- Handful of watercress
- 2 wholegrain crackerbread

Method

1 Add all the ingredients, except the crackerbread & watercress, to the NUTRiBULLET short cup. Be careful the ingredients don't go past the MAX line on your machine.

2 Twist on the NUTRiBULLET blade, turn the cup over and give it a tap down to make sure all the ingredients fall onto the blade.

3 Attach the short cup to the NUTRiBULLET power base and pulse for one second at a time to give you a textured/chopped dip. Don't blend for too long, as you don't want to puree the salmon.

4 Scoop out the dip from the cup and spoon onto the crackerbread with the watercress and plenty of salt & pepper.

CHEFS NOTE

Try using mayonnaise or cream cheese instead of yogurt if you like.

Skinny

MEALS IN MINUTES
SALAD
DRESSINGS

....

All these dressings will last you for four servings and will keep for at least a couple of days stored in a lidded jar in the fridge.

....

HONEY & PEPPER SALAD DRESSING

225 calories per serving

Ingredients

- 4 tbsp olive oil
- 4 roasted red peppers
- 4 garlic cloves, peeled
- 180ml/¾ cup fresh orange juice
- 2 tbsp honey
- Salt & pepper for seasoning

Method

1 Add all the ingredients to the NUTRiBULLET tall cup. Be careful the ingredients don't go past the MAX line on your machine.

2 Twist on the NUTRiBULLET blade, turn the cup over and give it a tap down to make sure all the ingredients fall onto the blade. Attach to the NUTRiBULLET power base and pulse until smooth.

3 Adjust the seasoning and serve.

CHEFS NOTE
Use jars of pre-roasted peppers.

SPICY ROCKET SALAD DRESSING

175 calories per serving

Ingredients

- 4 tbsp olive oil
- 100g/3½oz rocket
- 1 tbsp Dijon mustard
- 4 tbsp lemon juice
- 4 tbsp horseradish sauce
- 2 garlic cloves, peeled
- Salt & pepper for seasoning

SPICY !

Method

1 Add all the ingredients to the NUTRiBULLET tall cup. Be careful the ingredients don't go past the MAX line on your machine.

2 Twist on the NUTRiBULLET blade, turn the cup over and give it a tap down to make sure all the ingredients fall onto the blade. Attach to the NUTRiBULLET power base and pulse until smooth.

3 Adjust the seasoning and serve.

CHEFS NOTE
You could also use spinach for this dressing.

CUCUMBER YOGURT DRESSING

60 calories per serving

Ingredients

- Ingredients:
- 8 tbsp fat free Greek yogurt
- 1 cucumber, cut into thirds
- Large bunch of fresh mint
- 2 garlic cloves, peeled
- Salt & pepper for seasoning

Method

1 Add all the ingredients to the NUTRiBULLET tall cup. Be careful the ingredients don't go past the MAX line on your machine.

2 Twist on the NUTRiBULLET blade, turn the cup over and give it a tap down to make sure all the ingredients fall onto the blade. Attach to the NUTRiBULLET power base and pulse until smooth.

3 Adjust the seasoning and serve.

CHEFS NOTE
Try some fresh coriander and a twist of lemon with this dressing.

TANGY SALAD DRESSING

150 calories per serving

Ingredients

- 4 tbsp olive oil
- 4 tbsp balsamic vinegar
- Bunch of spring onions/scallions
- 4 tbsp ketchup

- 2 tsp English mustard
- 2 garlic cloves, peeled
- Salt & pepper for seasoning

Method

1 Add all the ingredients to the NUTRiBULLET tall cup. Be careful the ingredients don't go past the MAX line on your machine.

2 Twist on the NUTRiBULLET blade, turn the cup over and give it a tap down to make sure all the ingredients fall onto the blade. Attach to the NUTRiBULLET power base and pulse until smooth.

3 Adjust the seasoning and serve.

CHEFS NOTE

Make sure you get the balance of vinegar right. Add a pinch of brown sugar if you need to.

RASPBERRY VINAIGRETTE

SERVES 4

165 calories per serving

······· *Ingredients* ·······

- 4 tbsp olive oil
- 1 tbsp honey
- 60ml/¼ cup white wine vinegar
-
-
-

- 300g/11oz fresh raspberries
- Salt & pepper for seasoning

······· *Method* ·······

1 Add all the ingredients to the NUTRiBULLET tall cup. Be careful the ingredients don't go past the MAX line on your machine.

2 Twist on the NUTRiBULLET blade, turn the cup over and give it a tap down to make sure all the ingredients fall onto the blade. Attach to the NUTRiBULLET power base and pulse until smooth.

3 Adjust the seasoning and serve.

CHEFS NOTE
Frozen raspberries work just fine for this dressing too.

SIMPLE FRENCH SALAD DRESSING

170 calories per serving

Ingredients

- 4 tbsp olive oil
- 60ml/¼ cup white wine vinegar
- 1 tbsp Dijon mustard
- 1 tbsp tomato puree/paste
- 1 tbsp honey
- Bunch of spring onions/scallions
- Salt & pepper for seasoning

Method

1 Add all the ingredients to the NUTRiBULLET tall cup. Be careful the ingredients don't go past the MAX line on your machine.

2 Twist on the NUTRiBULLET blade, turn the cup over and give it a tap down to make sure all the ingredients fall onto the blade. Attach to the NUTRiBULLET power base and pulse until smooth.

3 Adjust the seasoning and serve.

CHEFS NOTE
Use shallots or a small piece of onion if you don't have spring onions.

CREAMY PARSLEY SALAD DRESSING

190 calories per serving

Ingredients

- 4 tbsp olive oil
- 4 tbsp white wine vinegar
- 8 tbsp fat free Greek yoghurt
- 2 garlic cloves, peeled
- Bunch of fresh flat leaf parsley
- Salt & pepper for seasoning

QUICK & EASY!

Method

1 Add all the ingredients to the NUTRiBULLET tall cup. Be careful the ingredients don't go past the MAX line on your machine.

2 Twist on the NUTRiBULLET blade, turn the cup over and give it a tap down to make sure all the ingredients fall onto the blade. Attach to the NUTRiBULLET power base and pulse until smooth.

3 Adjust the balance of the dressing and serve.

CHEFS NOTE
Season with plenty of salt and freshly ground black pepper.

CHILLI SWEET SOY DRESSING

180
calories per serving

Ingredients

- 4 tbsp olive oil
- 2 tsp sesame oil
- 4 tbsp lime juice
- 4 tbsp soy sauce
- 1 tbsp honey
- 1 red chilli, deseeded
- Salt & pepper for seasoning

Method

1 Add all the ingredients to the NUTRiBULLET tall cup. Be careful the ingredients don't go past the MAX line on your machine.

2 Twist on the NUTRiBULLET blade, turn the cup over and give it a tap down to make sure all the ingredients fall onto the blade. Attach to the NUTRiBULLET power base and pulse until smooth.

3 Adjust the balance of the dressing and serve.

CHEFS NOTE
This is good drizzled over slices of grilled chicken.

CITRUS CORIANDER DRESSING

165 calories per serving

Ingredients

- 4 tbsp olive oil
- 8 tbsp orange juice
- 4 tbsp lime juice
- 1 tbsp honey

- 1 tsp ground cumin
- Bunch of fresh coriander
- Salt & pepper for seasoning

Method

1 Add all the ingredients to the NUTRiBULLET tall cup. Be careful the ingredients don't go past the MAX line on your machine.

2 Twist on the NUTRiBULLET blade, turn the cup over and give it a tap down to make sure all the ingredients fall onto the blade. Attach to the NUTRiBULLET power base and pulse until smooth.

3 Adjust the balance of the dressing and serve.

CHEFS NOTE

You could add half an avocado to make a creamy version of this dressing.

MANGO & TOMATO DRESSING

185 calories per serving

Ingredients

USE A RIPE MANGO ➤

- 5 tbsp olive oil
- 1 mango, peeled & stoned
- 4 vine ripened tomatoes
- Salt & pepper for seasoning

Method

1 Add all the ingredients to the NUTRiBULLET tall cup. Be careful the ingredients don't go past the MAX line on your machine.

2 Twist on the NUTRiBULLET blade, turn the cup over and give it a tap down to make sure all the ingredients fall onto the blade. Attach to the NUTRiBULLET power base and pulse until smooth.

3 Adjust the balance of the dressing and serve.

CHEFS NOTE
You could add a handful of almonds or walnuts to this simple fruity dressing.

SWEET PEANUT BUTTER SALAD DRESSING

180 calories per serving

Ingredients

- 8 tbsp low fat peanut butter
- 4 tbsp water (add more if needed)
- 1 tbsp tomato puree/paste
- 1 tbsp honey
- Salt & pepper for seasoning

TRY AGAVE NECTAR

Method

1 Add all the ingredients to the NUTRiBULLET tall cup. Be careful the ingredients don't go past the MAX line on your machine.

2 Twist on the NUTRiBULLET blade, turn the cup over and give it a tap down to make sure all the ingredients fall onto the blade. Attach to the NUTRiBULLET power base and pulse until smooth.

3 Adjust the seasoning and serve.

CHEFS NOTE

Use smooth peanut butter for this dressing.

Other COOKNATION TITLES

If you enjoyed 'The NUTRiBULLET Meals In Minutes Recipe Book' we'd really appreciate your feedback. Reviews help others decide if this is the right book for them so a moment of your time would be appreciated.

Thank you.

You may also be interested in other 'Skinny' titles in the CookNation series. You can find all the following great titles by searching under 'CookNation'.

THE SKINNY SLOW COOKER RECIPE BOOK

Delicious Recipes Under 300, 400 And 500 Calories.

Paperback / eBook

THE SKINNY INDIAN TAKEAWAY RECIPE BOOK

Authentic British Indian Restaurant Dishes Under 300, 400 And 500 Calories. The Secret To Low Calorie Indian Takeaway Food At Home.

Paperback / eBook

THE HEALTHY KIDS SMOOTHIE BOOK

40 Delicious Goodness In A Glass Recipes for Happy Kids.

eBook

THE SKINNY 5:2 FAST DIET FAMILY FAVOURITES RECIPE BOOK

Eat With All The Family On Your Diet Fasting Days.

Paperback / eBook

THE SKINNY SLOW COOKER VEGETARIAN RECIPE BOOK

40 Delicious Recipes Under 200, 300 And 400 Calories.

Paperback / eBook

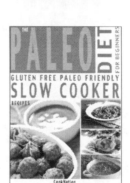

THE PALEO DIET FOR BEGINNERS SLOW COOKER RECIPE BOOK

Gluten Free, Everyday Essential Slow Cooker Paleo Recipes For Beginners.

eBook

THE SKINNY 5:2 SLOW COOKER RECIPE BOOK

Skinny Slow Cooker Recipe And Menu Ideas Under 100, 200, 300 & 400 Calories For Your 5:2 Diet.

Paperback / eBook

THE SKINNY 5:2 BIKINI DIET RECIPE BOOK

Recipes & Meal Planners Under 100, 200 & 300 Calories. Get Ready For Summer & Lose Weight...FAST!

Paperback / eBook

THE SKINNY 5:2 FAST DIET MEALS FOR ONE

Single Serving Fast Day Recipes & Snacks Under 100, 200 & 300 Calories.

Paperback / eBook

THE SKINNY HALOGEN OVEN FAMILY FAVOURITES RECIPE BOOK

Healthy, Low Calorie Family Meal-Time Halogen Oven Recipes Under 300, 400 and 500 Calories.

Paperback / eBook

THE SKINNY 5:2 FAST DIET VEGETARIAN MEALS FOR ONE

Single Serving Fast Day Recipes & Snacks Under 100, 200 & 300 Calories.

Paperback / eBook

THE PALEO DIET FOR BEGINNERS MEALS FOR ONE

The Ultimate Paleo Single Serving Cookbook.

Paperback / eBook

THE SKINNY SOUP MAKER RECIPE BOOK

Delicious Low Calorie, Healthy and Simple Soup Recipes Under 100, 200 and 300 Calories. Perfect For Any Diet and Weight Loss Plan.

Paperback / eBook

THE PALEO DIET FOR BEGINNERS HOLIDAYS

Thanksgiving, Christmas & New Year Paleo Friendly Recipes.
eBook

SKINNY HALOGEN OVEN COOKING FOR ONE

Single Serving, Healthy, Low Calorie Halogen Oven RecipesUnder 200, 300 and 400 Calories.

Paperback / eBook

SKINNY WINTER WARMERS RECIPE BOOK

Soups, Stews, Casseroles & One Pot Meals Under 300, 400 & 500 Calories.

Paperback / eBook

THE SKINNY 5:2 DIET RECIPE BOOK COLLECTION

All The 5:2 Fast Diet Recipes You'll Ever Need. All Under 100, 200, 300, 400 And 500 Calories.

eBook

THE SKINNY SLOW COOKER CURRY RECIPE BOOK

Low Calorie Curries From Around The World.

Paperback / eBook

THE SKINNY BREAD MACHINE RECIPE BOOK

70 Simple, Lower Calorie, Healthy Breads...Baked To Perfection In Your Bread Maker.

Paperback / eBook

MORE SKINNY SLOW COOKER RECIPES

75 More Delicious Recipes Under 300, 400 & 500 Calories.

Paperback / eBook

THE SKINNY 5:2 DIET CHICKEN DISHES RECIPE BOOK

Delicious Low Calorie Chicken Dishes Under 300, 400 & 500 Calories.

Paperback / eBook

THE SKINNY 5:2 CURRY RECIPE BOOK

Spice Up Your Fast Days With Simple Low Calorie Curries, Snacks, Soups, Salads & Sides Under 200, 300 & 400 Calories.

Paperback / eBook

THE SKINNY JUICE DIET RECIPE BOOK

5lbs, 5 Days. The Ultimate Kick- Start Diet and Detox Plan to Lose Weight & Feel Great!

Paperback / eBook

THE SKINNY SLOW COOKER SOUP RECIPE BOOK

Simple, Healthy & Delicious Low Calorie Soup Recipes For Your Slow Cooker. All Under 100, 200 & 300 Calories.

Paperback / eBook

THE SKINNY SLOW COOKER SUMMER RECIPE BOOK

Fresh & Seasonal Summer Recipes For Your Slow Cooker. All Under 300, 400 And 500 Calories.

Paperback / eBook

THE SKINNY HOT AIR FRYER COOKBOOK

Delicious & Simple Meals For Your Hot Air Fryer: Discover The Healthier Way To Fry.

Paperback / eBook

THE SKINNY ACTIFRY COOKBOOK

Guilt-free and Delicious ActiFry Recipe Ideas: Discover The Healthier Way to Fry!

Paperback / eBook

THE SKINNY ICE CREAM MAKER

Delicious Lower Fat, Lower Calorie Ice Cream, Frozen Yogurt & Sorbet Recipes For Your Ice Cream Maker.

Paperback / eBook

THE SKINNY 15 MINUTE MEALS RECIPE BOOK

Delicious, Nutritious & Super-Fast Meals in 15 Minutes Or Less. All Under 300, 400 & 500 Calories.

Paperback / eBook

THE SKINNY SLOW COOKER COLLECTION

5 Fantastic Books of Delicious, Diet-friendly Skinny Slow Cooker Recipes: ALL Under 200, 300, 400 & 500 Calories!
eBook

THE SKINNY MEDITERRANEAN RECIPE BOOK

Simple, Healthy & Delicious Low Calorie Mediterranean Diet Dishes. All Under 200, 300 & 400 Calories.

Paperback / eBook

THE SKINNY LOW CALORIE RECIPE BOOK

Great Tasting, Simple & Healthy Meals Under 300, 400 & 500 Calories. Perfect For Any Calorie Controlled Diet.

Paperback / eBook

THE SKINNY TAKEAWAY RECIPE BOOK

Healthier Versions Of Your Fast Food Favourites: All Under 300, 400 & 500 Calories.

Paperback / eBook

THE SKINNY NUTRIBULLET RECIPE BOOK

80+ Delicious & Nutritious Healthy Smoothie Recipes. Burn Fat, Lose Weight and Feel Great!

Paperback / eBook

THE SKINNY NUTRIBULLET SOUP RECIPE BOOK

Delicious, Quick & Easy, Single Serving Soups & Pasta Sauces For Your Nutribullet. All Under 100, 200, 300 & 400 Calories!

Paperback / eBook

THE SKINNY PRESSURE COOKER COOKBOOK

USA ONLY
Low Calorie, Healthy & Delicious Meals, Sides & Desserts. All Under 300, 400 & 500 Calories.

Paperback / eBook

THE SKINNY ONE-POT RECIPE BOOK

Simple & Delicious, One-Pot Meals. All Under 300, 400 & 500 Calories

Paperback / eBook

CONVERSION CHART: DRY INGREDIENTS

Metric	Imperial
7g	¼ oz
15g	½ oz
20g	¾ oz
25g	1 oz
40g	1½oz
50g	2oz
60g	2½oz
75g	3oz
100g	3½oz
125g	4oz
140g	4½oz
150g	5oz
165g	5½oz
175g	6oz
200g	7oz
225g	8oz
250g	9oz
275g	10oz
300g	11oz
350g	12oz
375g	13oz
400g	14oz

Metric	Imperial
425g	15oz
450g	1lb
500g	1lb 2oz
550g	1¼lb
600g	1lb 5oz
650g	1lb 7oz
675g	1½lb
700g	1lb 9oz
750g	1lb 11oz
800g	1¾lb
900g	2lb
1kg	2¼lb
1.1kg	2½lb
1.25kg	2¾lb
1.35kg	3lb
1.5kg	3lb 6oz
1.8kg	4lb
2kg	4½lb
2.25kg	5lb
2.5kg	5½lb
2.75kg	6lb